C...... ON DEMAND

ROYSTON ROBERTSON

To my parents this time, for
encouraging me to draw

All contents © Royston Robertson 2014

All rights reserved. No part of this publication may
be reproduced, stored in or introduced into a retrieval
system, or transmitted, in any form, or by any means
(electronic, mechanical, photocopying, recording or
otherwise) without the prior written permission of the
author. Any person who does any unauthorised act in
relation to this publication may be liable to criminal
prosecution and civil claims for damages

ISBN 978-1-304-95466-4

Also available:
*Penguin vs Polar Bear and
Other Ridiculous Cartoons*

www.roystoncartoons.com

People often assume that the bulk of my work as a cartoonist is coming up with topical, up-to-the-minute jokes. That is part of the job, of course, but most of my gag cartoons are more about simply reflecting the way we live now. So it's inevitable that as a result I seem to do rather a lot of jokes about technology.

Like most people, I like computers and smartphones when they work. The rest of the time – quite a lot of the time – I like to shout at them. Happily, I also have the outlet of drawing cartoons about them.

I hope you enjoy this new collection. The cartoons are not *all* about technology, there are a lot more subjects covered, but they have all appeared in the pages of *Private Eye*, *Prospect*, *Reader's Digest*, *The Spectator*, *The Oldie*, *Saga*, *New Humanist* and other magazines.

Royston

HOW COMPUTERS HAVE CHANGED

"I don't think you're supposed to use Google Earth"

"We believe this woman to be a witch as she is known to have expressed an opinion online"

"This is for all the things you have already heard about via Twitter"

"It's a battle of wills – I'm refusing to do anything funny for his YouTube page"

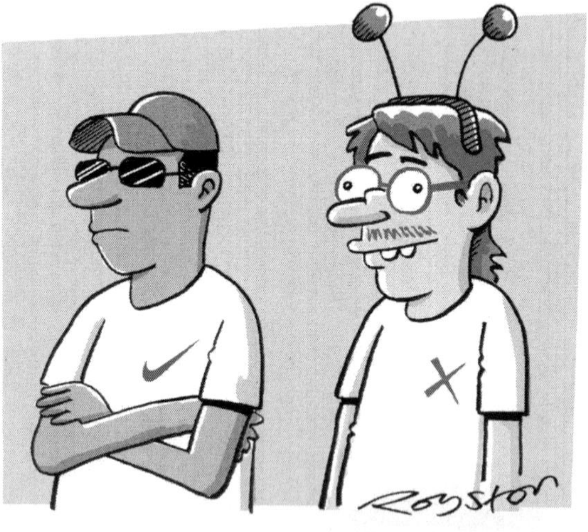
Royston

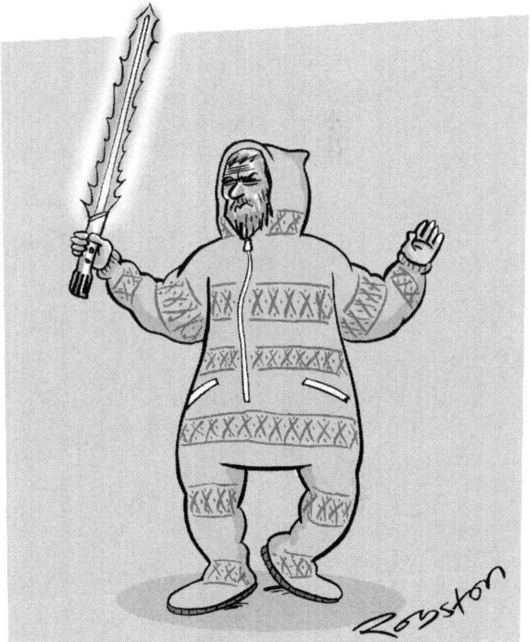

OBI-ONESIE KENOBI

"You're closing off potential career paths if you define yourself only as an impaler"

"Accurs'd stag nights!"

"How many units of alcohol do you kid yourself that you consume weekly?"

NANNY STATE GONE MAD...
It's not big and it's not clever
You'll stunt your growth
I can smell it on your breath, you know
You haven't just let me down, you've let yourself down
Royston

"It's black pudding – I'm trying to quit"

"I miss the angry mob – they must be at home criticising you on Twitter again"

"Zombies! The worst kind ..."

"I'm just going outside ... you can follow me on Twitter"

"Look at him, with his head in the Cloud"

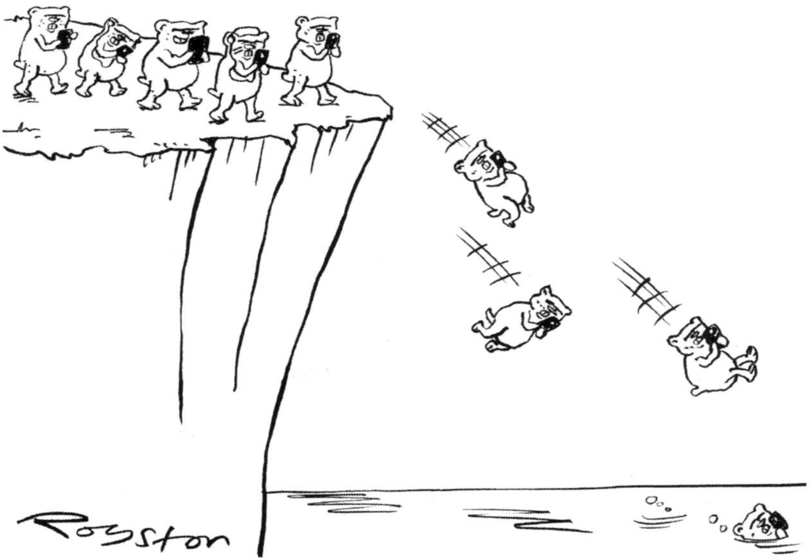
Royston

"We've got TV on demand"

"I'm going to set this lot up – will contain scenes that some may find upsetting and strong language throughout"

"You work from home? Me neither"

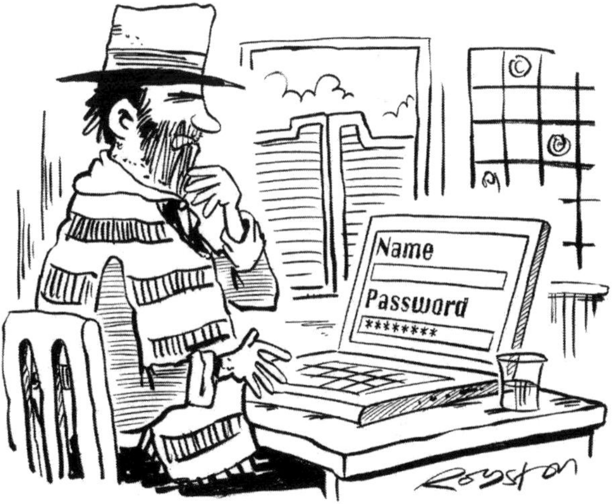
Name
Password
****
Royston

"Well, well, if it ain't the Limbo Kid..."

"This town ain't big enough for the two of us, so I'm proposing a thousand new homes with a commitment to affordable housing plus adjacent retail park and leisure destination"

"Welcome to Hell"

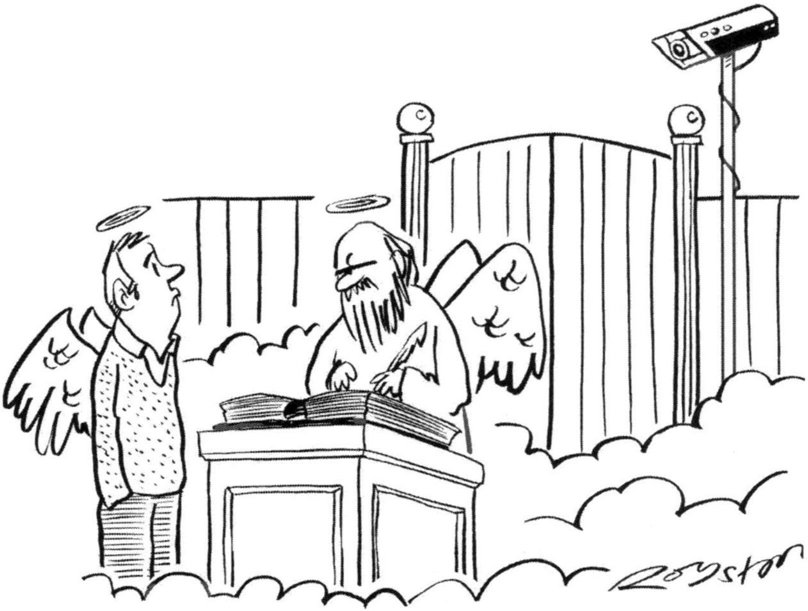
Royston

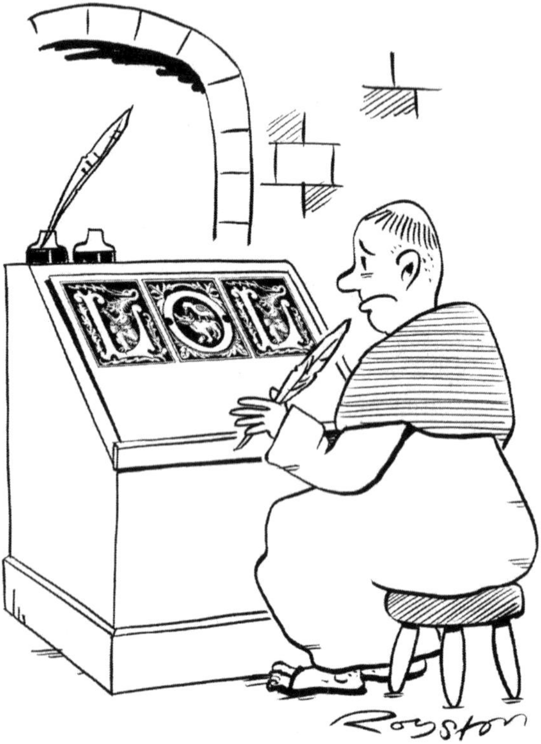
Royston

"He only got this job because of who his dad is"

"Oh no, I lost two followers"

"Run! It's the Higgs bison!"

"The new apprentice is here"

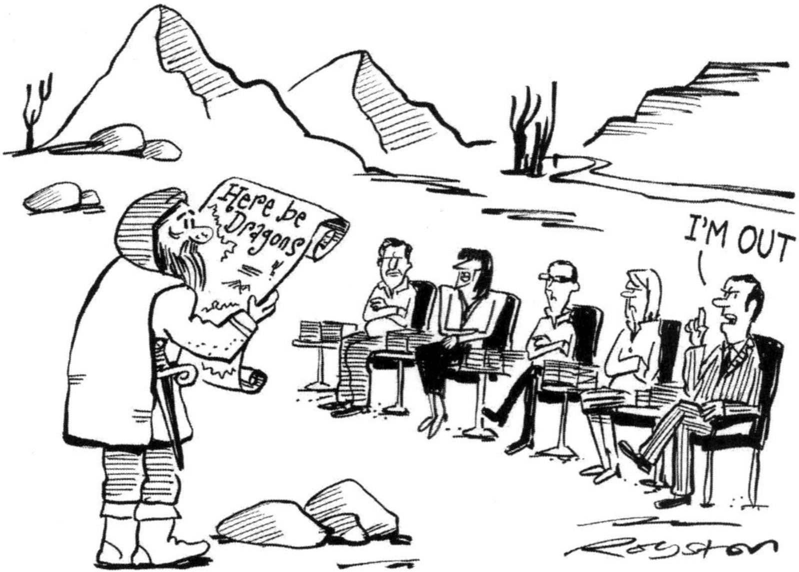
Here be Dragons
I'M OUT
Royston

"Hey, that one looks just like a visible mass of condensed water vapour floating in the atmosphere"

"We'll be seeing appalling shorts throughout the country and scattered outbreaks of ill-advised vests"

"How come we never get invited to these extreme weather events?"

"Calm down, it's helping me pay for all this"

"Times are hard, I've had to take in a lodger"

"I've lost count of how many times I've had to turn that kid away"

"Don't worry, I've called I.T. support …"

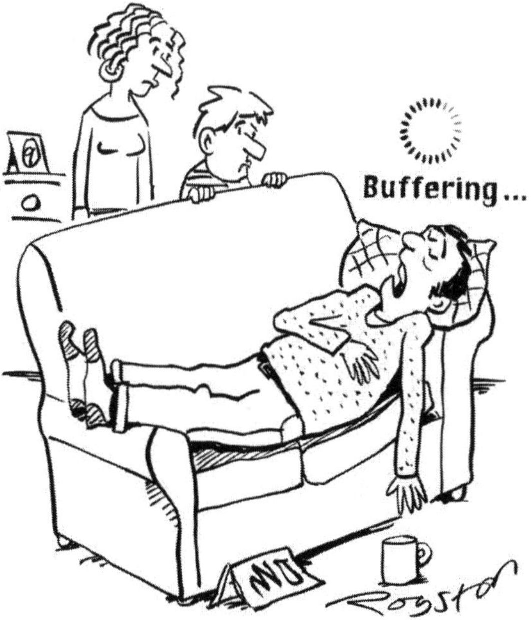
Buffering...
Royston

"Some blue-arsed fly you turned out to be"

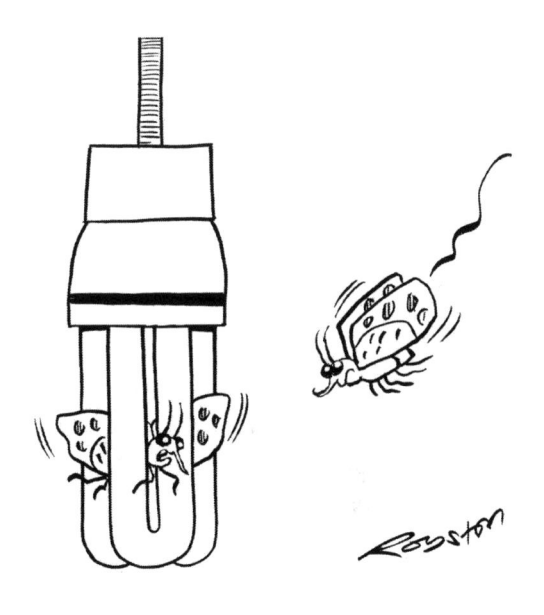

"This never used to happen in the old days"

"Must dash ... I want to spend some time on my social-networking sites"

"Don't look – I think it's my cyber-stalker"

"Do you ever get a hollow feeling when you've looked forward to something for ages and it finally happens?"

A GLIMPSE OF THE FUTURE...
SO SHE WAS LIKE, NO WAAY!
AN' I'M, LIKE, WHA' EVA!!
OMG!
AWESOME!
ROYSTON

"Once I tried on those clothes at your Grandma's house, I knew there was no going back"

"Ohmigod, what big ears she has! Ohmigod, what a big nose she has ..."

BOOKS
NO BATTERIES REQUIRED!
WORKS IN SUNLIGHT!
CAN BE JUDGED BY COVER!
Royston

"It's tough to admit that now I will never own a bookcase which springs open to reveal a hidden room"

"No, I'm not on Twitter. If you must know,
I'm browsing the FT website."

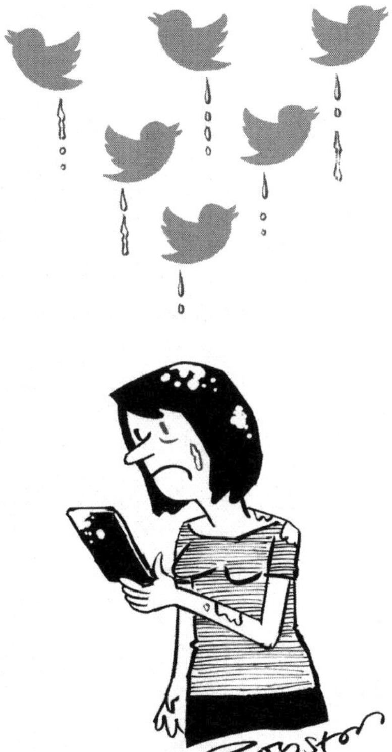
Royston

"'Appy darling?"

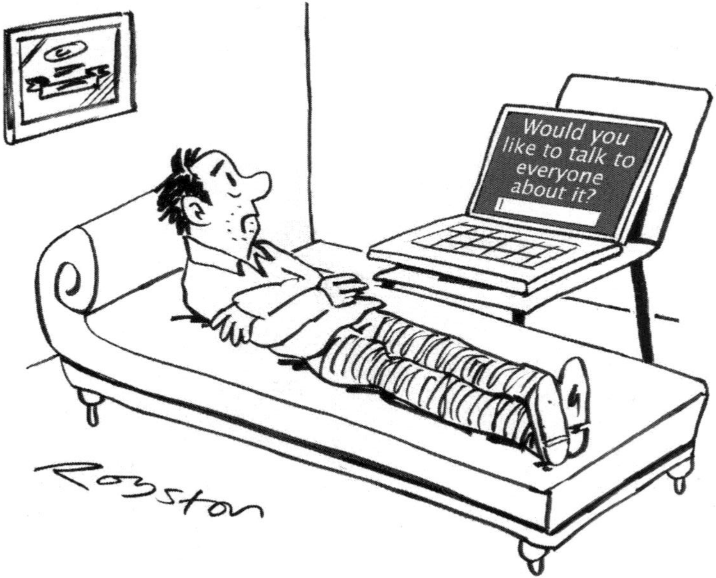
Would you like to talk to everyone about it?
Royston

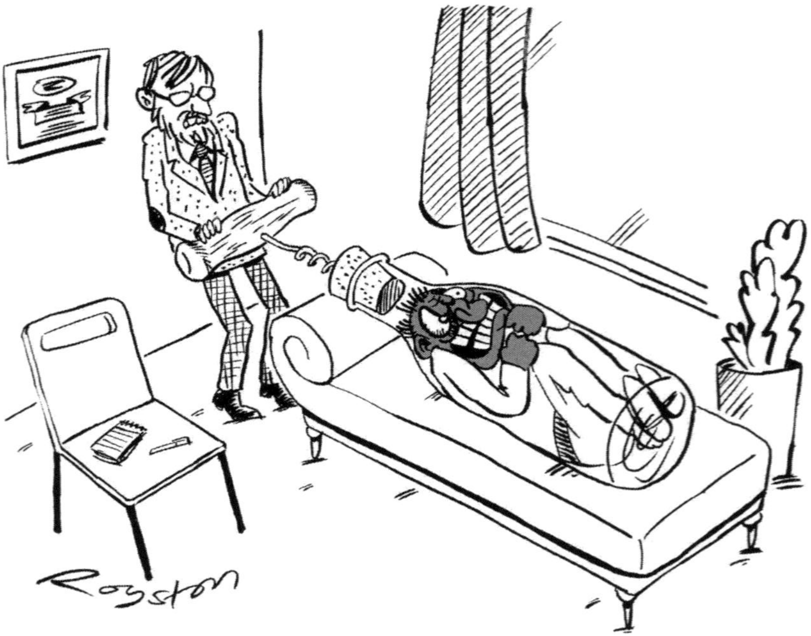
Royston

"Do you think, perhaps, you are really angry at yourself?"

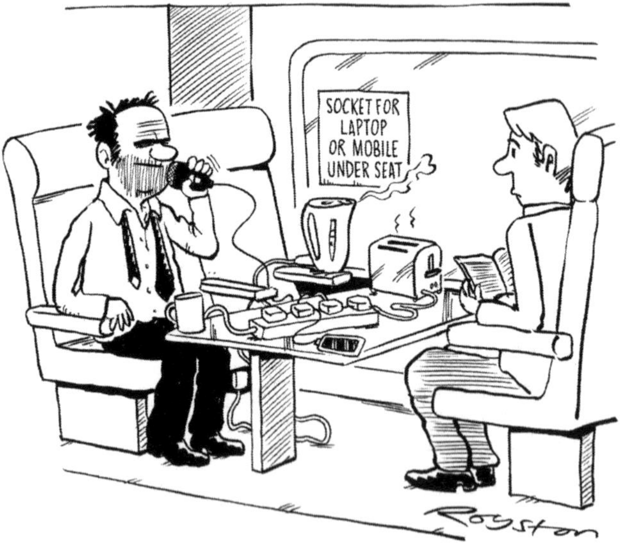
SOCKET FOR
LAPTOP
OR MOBILE
UNDER SEAT
Royston

"Please keep all your belongings with you at all times"

"These days it's called crowdfunding"

YOU NEED FRESH AIR AND EXERCISE
IS THERE A BOX-SET OF IT?
PIZZA
ROYSTON

"I'm rehashing an old magazine piece about how popular culture keeps revisiting the past"

"You know what they say: if you can remember the Sixties then talk about them endlessly on BBC Four documentaries"

"Forget whalesong, I'm giving them
some thrash metal"

"We're very excited about this cashback, er, I mean comeback, tour"

Hear no evil, hear no evil, hear no evil

"We're all having to work harder in
the music business now"

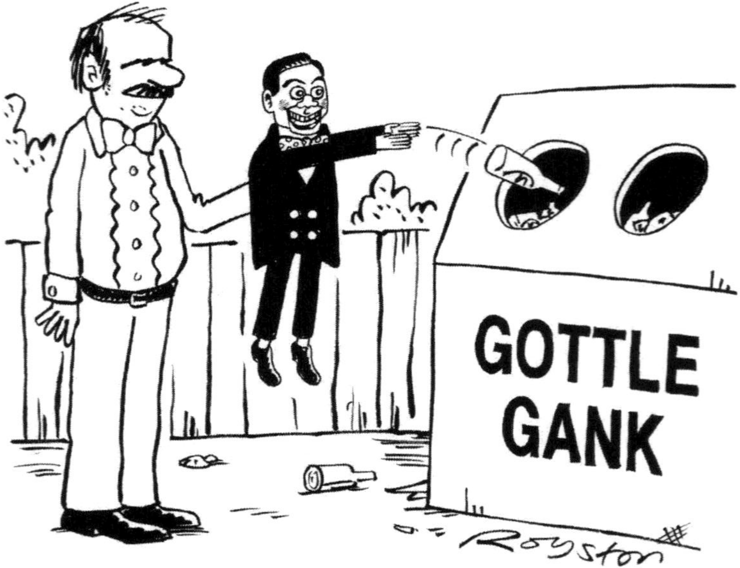
GOTTLE GANK
Royston

"I'm not being funny, right, but ..."

"I'm not being racist, right, but ..."

"Don't fill up with bread"

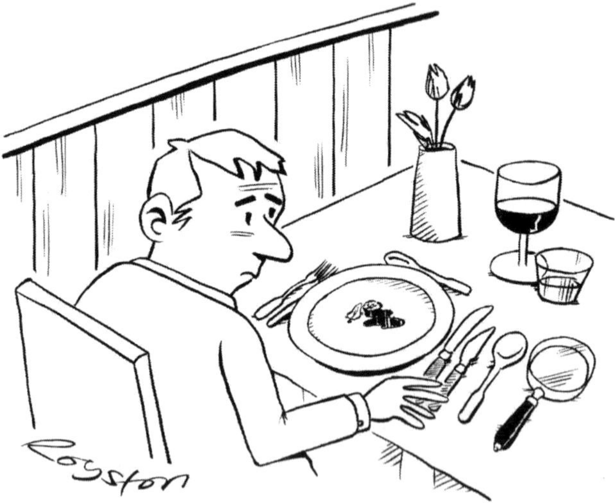
Royston

"You shouldn't eat foods that are out of season"

"Hey, this vintage coat has still got a vintage person inside it"

The man who bought a sofa that was not in a sale

"Men and their sheds, eh?"

"Typical man – why can't he just ask for directions?"

"That may not be the best option for printing out your novel"

THANK YOU
for not saying
*Can you do
mine next?
*It'll rain now
*Missed a bit
Royston

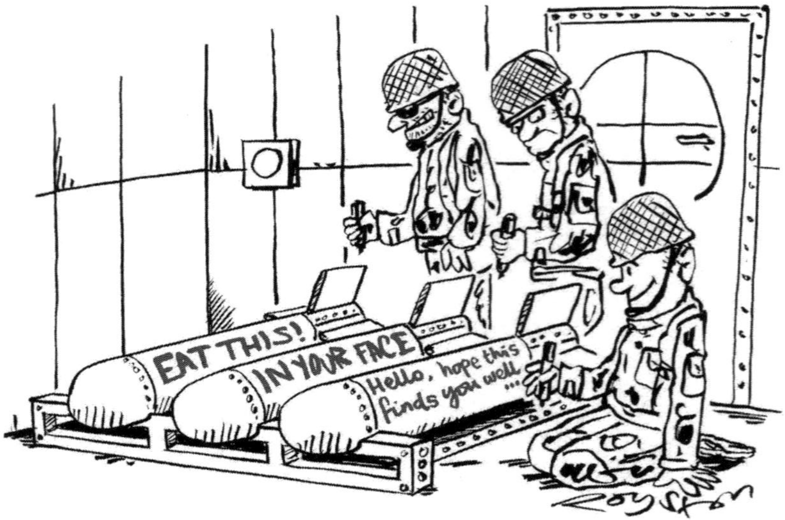
EAT THIS!
IN YOUR FACE
Hello, hope this finds you well ...
ROYSTON

"You say comedy catchphrase, the law says bomb threat"

I PRESSED THE FIRE CONTROL... AND AHEAD OF ME ROCKETS BLAZED THROUGH THE SKY...
DAAMN!
...THAT WAS ONE OF OUR GUYS!
Royston
with apologies

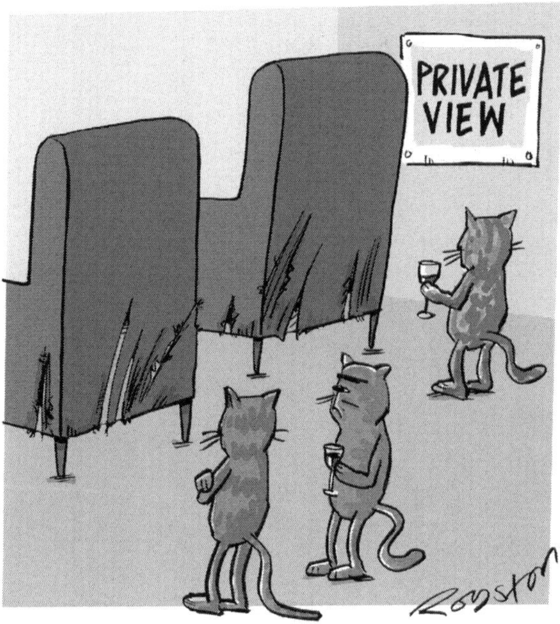
PRIVATE
VIEW

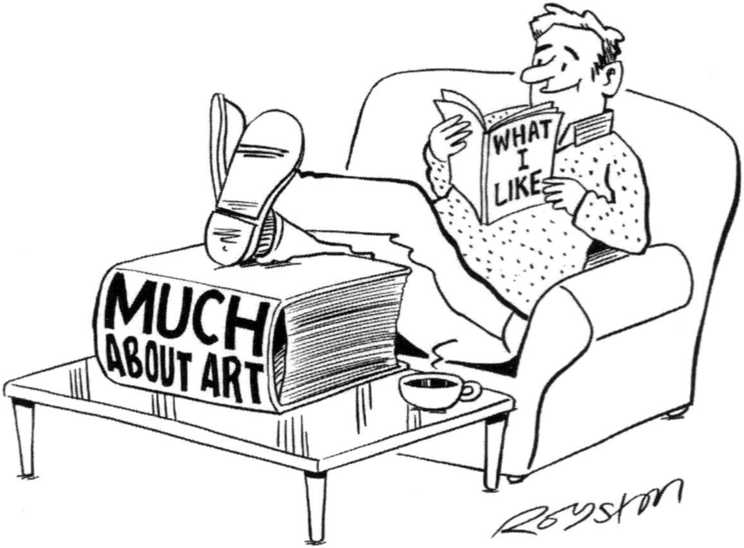
WHAT I LIKE
MUCH ABOUT ART
Royston

"No! It picture of hunt! It not 'really about inner conflict' ..."

"I'm in hunting mostly but I dabble in gathering"

"Barbarians at the gate? That's fine, I fully support social mobility"

"Unexpected Spanish Inquisition in bagging area ..."

"Sire, the risk-assessment people say: No way"

"How satisfied are you with the service you have received today? Very satisfied, satisfied, neutral ..."

"Honestly, I live here but I forgot my key"

"This is your idea of quality father-son time?"

"For the last time, it's not stocks, it's a pillory"

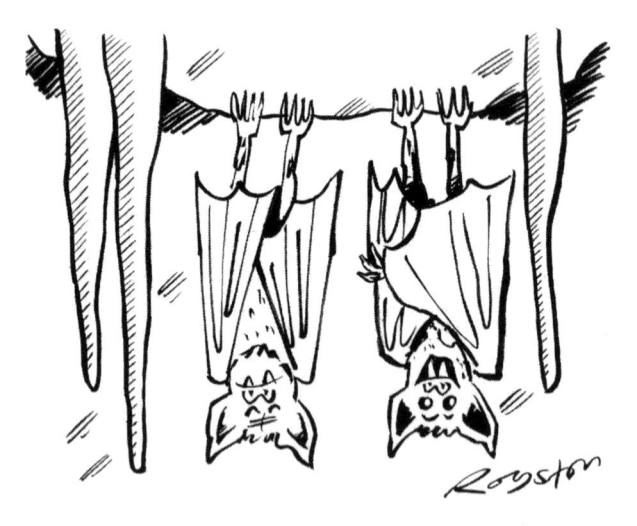

"If you could have any super power, what would it be?"

"I refuse to be pigeonholed"

FICTION
TWO FOR ONE OFFER
The Girl with the Dragon Tattoo and a Pearl Earring
Royston

WILL NEVER BE FINISHED
AIN'T GONNA HAPPEN
NOPE
WHO ARE YOU KIDDING?
NOT A CHANCE
Royston

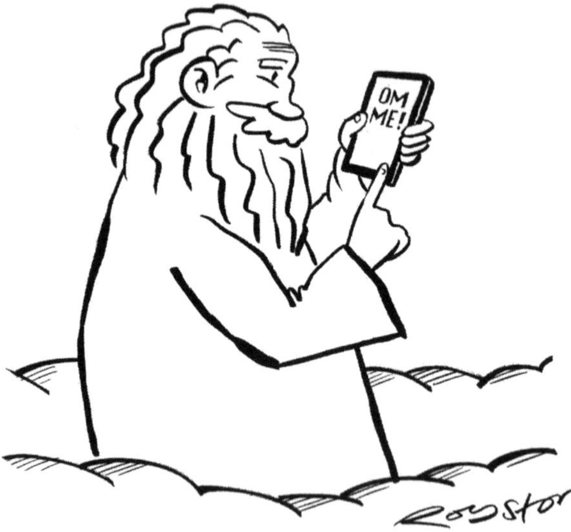
OM
ME!
Royston

*"It's the golden rule of the computer age:
If it ain't broke, upgrade it"*

WITH SMARTPHONES YOU NEED TO MASTER THE SWIPING MOTION
..., LIKE SO
Royston

To see more cartoons by Royston, visit
roystoncartoons.com

And there's more at
roystonrobertson.co.uk

Should you wish to, you can find him
on Twitter as **@roystoncartoons**

And, with some inevitability, at
Facebook.com/roystoncartoons

Ask about buying prints and original
artwork, or you can commission Royston to
draw custom-made cartoons

His first book *Penguin vs Polar Bear
and Other Ridiculous Cartoons*
is also available